Art, Inequity and Technological Ubiquity

Joslyn Lundie

An imprint of Boom Publications Ltd

272 Bath Street
Glasgow SCOTLAND
G2 4JR

Boom Graduates and the logo are trademarks of Boom Publications Ltd.

Boom Publications Ltd is a more-than-profit company, dedicating over half our profits to university scholarships for underprivileged students worldwide. In order to offset our carbon footprint, we also pledge to plant a tree for each graduation book commissioned.

Art, Inequity and Technological Ubiquity
was first published in Great Britain in 2022.

Copyright © Joslyn Lundie. Joslyn Lundie has asserted her right under the Copyright, Designs and Patents Act, 1988,
to be identified as Author of this work.
For legal purposes any Acknowledgements constitute
an extension of this copyright page.
Cover design by Boom Graduates Ltd and the Book Cover Zone USA.

All rights are reserved. No part of this publication may be reproduced or transmitted in any form or by any means, electronic or mechanical, including photocopying, recording, or any information storage or retrieval system, without prior permission in writing from the publishers.
Boom Publications Ltd do not have any control over, or responsibility for any third-party websites referred to or in this book. All internet addresses given in this book were correct at the time of going to press. The author and publisher regret any inconvenience if addresses have changed or sites have ceased to exist, but can accept no responsibility for any such changes.

Typeset by Helen at Boom Graduates.
Printed and bound in the UK.
To find out more about our authors and books visit www.boomgraduates.com
and sign up for our newsletters.

Art, Inequity and Technological Ubiquity

We plant a tree for every
Boom Graduate book commissioned, and
thereafter plant a tree for every 10 books sold!

THG
(more : trees)

MEMBER

Watch our forest grow at
https://moretrees.eco/forest/BoomPublicationsLtd/

Joslyn Lundie

Art, Inequity and Technological Ubiquity

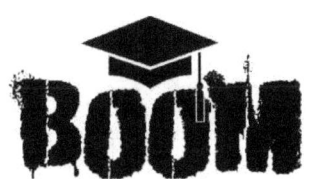

Joslyn Lundie

Contents

Author biography 9
Abstract 11
Introduction 13
Chapter 1 17
Chapter 2 33
Chapter 3 45
Conclusion 59
Bibliography 63
Artist's images 71
Acknowledgements 83
A note about Boom Graduates 85
BOOM! 89
Notes 91

Joslyn Lundie

Author biography

In her creative practice, Joslyn Lundie conceptually investigates branches of philosophical anthropology through various mediums. This book is an exploration into a theme Joslyn frequently ponders, a deeper look into how technological means and modern advancements have changed the art world and humanities' experiences with art. *Art, Inequity and Technological Ubiquity* delves into the bleary inequity that thrives in art because of a furthering of technological methods. It foregrounds how beneath these apparent advances in technology in art, be they social, economic or political, lays a general unequal hierarchy in humanity.

Joslyn Lundie

Abstract

This book forms an exploration into how technological means and modern advancements have changed the art world and humanity's experiences with art; it delves into the bleary inequity that thrives in art because of a furthering of technological methods. It foregrounds how beneath these apparent advances in technology in art, be they social, economic or political, lays a general unequal hierarchy in humanity. In three main chapters, this thesis depicts troublesome findings of technology and art supported by sources such as books, scholarly articles, artists and thinkers on the subject. The first chapter considers pioneering art movements that use technology as early as the 1960s, appreciating that technology can be a valuable tool in light of creating innovative art and driving growing interaction with the public through art. The second chapter inspects the ingrained hierarchy and inequality attributed to technological means and how art falls victim to facilitating this, creating problems in gender visibility, specifically for women. The third and final chapter considers current affairs in art and technology movements today, depicting the bleak reality of its effects as a tool in furthering inequity generally, minimising auratic experiences with the arts culture, and then looks at current art movements that exacerbate topical issues, such as climate change degradation.

Introduction

> The art market knows only unwritten laws and is rife with murky going on. The picture of a close-knit secretive community reluctant to reveal its practices is regularly evoked. –
>
> Isabelle Graw (Gorrill, 2019, p.166)

Isabelle Graw affirms in the book *Women Can't Paint: Gender, the Glass Ceiling and Values* by Helen Gorrill that we live amongst an art world built on inequity; this basis of unequal standards is already prominently ingrained and mirrors inequalities in society (Gorrill, 2019). As art follows the 'unwritten' rules created by those who primarily sit at the top, society also conforms to social hierarchy, driven and perpetuated by the accelerating technological lifestyle in contemporary modernity. The passive acceptance of ingrained inequality can be arguably furthered by technology and who has control – the affluent

Western world, predominantly male and white, who run corporations that aid technological advancements in the name of capitalism, for instance (Alegria, 2020). Technology is currently an underlay of economic, social and political changes, meaning it helps rapidly shape everything we know and how we know it (Haig, 2019). With the ubiquitous use of technology, we can evermore look at the art world as a microcosm for insight into society's conformant behavioural and emotional changes. These conformant behavioural and emotional changes are caused by the distraction and distortion of reality through technological approaches to virtual viewing. Electronic and mechanical technological roots lie within elitist, for-profit motives, creating a reality that is not always best for humankind or the planet (Alegria, 2020). With this realisation, we have arrived at a ubiquitous technological crossroad. Regularly showing negativistic perspectives, it can be argued that the art world is not as it once was, with many technological movements and advancements in art furthering already ingrained divisions in social hierarchies in the industry, dimming real-life experiences in the arts and culture and favouring capitalism within art (Margulis et al., 2019). The arts' interactions with technological advancements today can be deprived of evoking emotion within its viewers, a theme we see appear in the world principally entrenched with technology generally; this is arguably due to distractions of online activity and the digital physicality of reproduced images, never fully allowing submersion into the essence and scale of physical artworks that are viewed online. Distractions within technological use is a subject that has been researched and concluded to be true, depicting that 'media multitasking' is something accessibly done on devices which allow multiple web pages open, such as with laptops and mobile devices (Gazzaley et al., 2016). Art falls victim to technological advancements governed by the social hierarchy, including further problems in recurring issues, such as gender visibility, art satisfying capitalist motives and our dulled experiences with art in a ubiquitous technological world. This thesis is an exploration of some significant technological changes and challenges within three chapters that reflect on technology and art. The chapters that follow will explore pioneering movements in art and technological advancements such as Cybernetics and Network Art, the female artist and her visibility in use of technological mediums, and the current contemporary art world's utilisation of technology more recently, showing furthering inequality and exacerbating an impaired aura through experience with the arts' lack of physicality and arousing impacts online.

Chapter 1

Prosperous Art in the Emergence of Technological Advancement

Although art with technology has an eerie impassiveness in recent times, it is still undoubtedly accurate that "We find ourselves surrounded by echoes of technology in our public and private lives" as Tom Corby notes in the book *Network Art*; he is known professor within the arts and working artist, exploring technological mediums (Corby, 2006 p.25). We use technology daily as a quick fix for monotonous amusement and distraction. This distraction and lack of attention are furthered with addictions to smartphones that daily swamp us as "studies have shown that 95 percent of the population report media multitasking each day"

(Gazzaley et al., 2016 p.11). This will not change, with smartphones and laptops presently ingrained in almost every aspect of life. However, this is not to say art and technological interactions have always furthered impassiveness that clings to technological use, and that technology and art cannot successfully coexist today or in the future – changes must be made to our relationship with technology and who has access to it, which ultimately boils down to ingrained equity, ever-present.

Earlier art movements effectively demonstrate that technological attributes can be consciously grasped for clear potential purposefully and demonstrate technology's advantages through stimulating and pioneering art movements, such as Cybernetic Art and Network Art, also known as Net Art. The more engaging impact in these particular movements may be due to the lack of control and presence during the development of these art movements of technologies, creating familiarly bathetic feelings evoked in other forms of technological consumption today. Cybernetic Art and Network Art are two art movements that help depict art through a paramount aesthetic concerned with what technology and art can successfully create, noted in earlier advancements. These early technological movements arguably wanted to show an understanding and appreciation for new developments in technology. It undeniably educated technological advancements publicly. That is not to say the monetary value was not an objective for those involved with these movements but seemingly a minor motive in juxtaposition to today's ideals regarding art and technology, where capital gain is arguably the primary aim. In movements like the Cybernetics movement, gratifying technologically based art exhibitions and works could be witnessed for the first time on a large scale, publicly giving the world of art recognition for their advancements in technological uses as early as the 1960s. This is evident in one of the first constructive exhibitions to show art and technology could correlate and is of public interest as we have seen in the exhibition *Cybernetic Serendipity,* as it demonstrated to artists and the public the potential for uses of technology as a medium:

> Attracting the attention of the national and international press at the time, *Cybernetic Serendipity* was the first international exhibition in the UK devoted to the relationship between the arts and new technology. This ground-breaking exhibition, designed by Franciszka Themerson, presented the work of over 130 participants including composers, engineers, artists, mathematicians and poets. The exhibition ran from 2 August - 20 October 1968 and was seen by some 60,000 visitors
>
> (Reichardt, 2014).

This exhibition indicated some indisputable evidence that technology did create some of the most advanced and, arguably, interesting artworks the world has ever seen; the display was recognised for its garnered public interest and innovation. Cybernetics in machines substantially birthed ground-breaking access to communication possibilities through technological advancements in art. Artists placed their feasibility for transcending presence in the art world through experimentations seen in the exhibition, allowing art to move with technological advances. It redefined what art could effectively do for humanity by pioneering space for communication with technology through the use of art; possibilities for interactive art grew with the *Cybernetics Serendipity* exhibition and the movement:

> Visitors could use huge magnets to stretch and distort the images on Nam June Paik's installation of 11 TV sets. They could whistle into a microphone and hear a variation of their tune played back by Zinovieff's computerised recording studio exhibit. Many were charmed by the flower-like sculpture SAM (Sound Activated Mobile), which would rotate towards you when you spoke to it.
>
> (Evans-Pughe, 2018).

It is vital to validate technological encounters such as this one that helped construct how art would shift onto more advanced ways to communicate the concepts and ideas of artists. Technology was, and can still be, a beneficial medium. Cybernetics paved the way for a new kind of technological art world as recognised here with the early generation of artists who used technologies to create within the movement; they are said to have "subsequently laid the foundation for decades of advancement in the arenas of digital image-making, animation, interactivity, intermedia and cross-disciplinary collaboration in the arts, which is a feature of much contemporary art today" (Mason, 2018).

In many ways, technology, as we see it today, is unbelievably sophisticated; we live amongst unprecedented technological advancements. We can see the growth in audiences of technological art forms that began in movements like Cybernetics. Yet, technology's possible advantage today compared to when the Cybernetic movement came about, is its increased accessibility, making technology more widespread for artists to create with. For example, Cybernetics was considered to be "highly dependent on support and funding" (Mason, 2018) as a result of "the expensive, large-scale nature of much early equipment and the resulting technical expertise required to operate it" (Mason, 2018). Thus, there was a lack of accessibility to technology during its development, such as the period when Cybernetics and art merged. However, even with the advantage above of today's encounters with technology in the art world compared to these previous times, such as growth in accessibility, we can still easily comprehend a darker shift in current technological trends within the art world, as well as a depictable link to avaricious behaviour through the use of new technologies with art. These recognised avaricious feelings are evident in a branch of art concepts created based on "Post-Capital" life (Mudam, 2021). Artworks that help convey and reinforce the legitimacy of feeling towards this excessive overuse of technology and how it has created bleak realities can be depicted in the art exhibition held in Luxemburg called "Post-Capital Art and the Economics of the Digital Age" (Mudam, 2021), which is an exhibition that includes works by artists such as Hito Steyerl, who is also a filmmaker and writer known for her book *Duty Free Art: Art in the Age of Planetary Civil War*, described by *The Guardian* as a book that

"Poses uncomfortable questions about today's image culture and the art market" (Steyerl, 2017). Artist Cao Fai also contributed to the exhibition; as one of China's best-known multimedia artists. She has created works based on the iniquitousness of capitalist life and dark technological concepts (Fei, 2018).

Asia One is an artwork featured within the exhibition; the film follows the lives lived by the only two human employees who work amongst advanced machinery in a warehouse with an AI robot alongside them (Fai, 2018). The film turns to the interconnection of the female and male workers after conforming to the isolating life that develops when surrounded by automation and technology in the warehouse; a relationship blossoms that surpasses the need to adhere to the tedious lifestyle they lived (Fai, 2018). Concepts that have risen from post-capitalism life, such as this, usually follow a similar nature of closeting reality that is not a coincidence. A general theory is that technology and its rapid distracting nature can create a bleak, unfulfilling reality with excessive fear; Haig exercises this point for a conditioning need of anxiety and depression in society, which helps us become consumers to fulfil happiness (Haig, 2015).

Contentment where technology and art again show innovation and a more consummating reality is the Network Art movement, stemming from the introduction of the Worldwide Web in the early 1990s (Corby, 2006). Network Artists using the web saw possibilities of having their voice heard. as Corby states, "When 'user-friendly' web browsers such as *Mosaic* and *Netscape* came out in the early to mid-1990s, the possibilities of the web as a medium was seized upon by several artists, who started producing work under the banner of 'net art'" (Corby, 2006, p.20). Network Art had to adapt from the similar aspiring concept that Cybernetics had begun; that art and technology could be outstanding. Network Art showed the possibilities in technology and its advancements. It created an accessible bridge for a wider spread of voices for artists and their work. And "Following the invention of the World Wide Web and the ready availability of cheap computers, the number of people connecting to the internet soared" (Corby, 2006, p.70).

The Net Art movement became prevalent starting with a small group of artists creating on the Internet in 1996 and branding their work as "net art" (Corby, 2006, p. 68). This move allowed the freedom of ideas and speech through art in a technological world that was less restricting than governed reality at the time, which meant that "In 'Cyberspace', individuals would soar through information unencumbered by physical obstructions and government controls" (Corby, 2006, p.69). Freedom in the early use of the web was viewed as a reaction to the creation of advancements in the way we globally networked with the web. In Eastern Europe, with the collapse of the Soviet Union, people essentially turned to the possibilities of how a communal virtual space could help them powerfully respond with art and activism. People grasped the concept of the avant-garde (Tunali, 2016) through depicting artists and activists' milieux in new ways that differed from longstanding movements.

Here we can see how artists approached the power of networking, such as Eastern Europeans did, a tool combined with art to spread and portray their political feelings and thoughts with the possibility of worldwide interaction:

> The possibilities of exchange in the networked commons have revitalised collectivist strategies by providing new ways of interconnecting individuals and groups, as well as new means of challenging established structures of governance and power.
>
> (Paul, 2006).

As is evident in the above citation, the network was a way to connect new types of interest to participate in technology as a way to popularise freedom of ideas. This idea was adapted within art using the properties of the net. Internationally renowned Turkish art critic and curator, Beral Madra, points out that contemporary artists embraced cyberspace without having to apply self-censorship as "Artists, curators, critics who have been suffering under institutional conservatisms were looking to acquire skills to bypass them" (Tunali, 2016).

This writing about net artists by Beral Madra helps demonstrate contemporary artists' use of the web. Furthermore, it showed that art conforming somewhat to technological advancements in the times of the development of the internet helped pave the way for artists' voices to be heard in light of technological evolution. This realisation of what the power of networking online could do is undoubtedly essential. It shows artists understand the success of using a technological tool, such as the internet, to undertake activism through art efficaciously. As cited in the Cybernetics movement, the use of early technology was expensive in its early developments and usually attached to those who had technical expertise (Mason, 2018). However, net art through the online platform allowed something positively ubiquitous, a space in which freedom of thought could be widely used.

The internet enabled people to quickly connect without the need for extensive technical knowledge. An example of an artwork that subsequently depicts how net art has informed activism in a boundless and uncovering degree on the web's freeing space was 1998's DissemiNET work (Stryker et al., 1998). The work by Beth Stryker and Sawad Brooks allowed those in similar diaspora to make connections in an online environment, capable of mapping links between personal memories of stories; it allowed a collaborating space in which people could add and extract input from those who use the site (Stryker et al., 1998). It is noted on the DissemiNET website:

> Drawing parallels between diasporas and the dispersal of meaning over the web, DissemiNET provides spaces for people to recall and recollect, gathering there to re-tell stories about their own experiences with homelessness and dispersal.
>
> (Stryker et al., 1998).

DissemiNET aims to "act as a broadcast mechanism, disseminating these stories" (Stryker et al., 1998) and using the web allows such circulation and detection, following crucial themes seen in the Network Art movement and their concepts. It is vital to mention that Network Art is not all about activism. However, it coincides nicely with the instrument of spreading ideologies and information that activism relies on. It is also essential to validate that Network Art is not only online and can be seen in galleries and installation through different constructs. It is pivotal to account why Cybernetic Art and Network Art are plausible for their technological uses, unlike art frequently found and created through technology today. The difference in this is a factor regarding heightening "Digital Dictatorship" (Rozpedowski, 2021) through surveillance and growth in government control of our online activity as mentioned herewith, which are menacing uses for the technology:

> Scholars speculate that a prospective data arms race in AI, robotics, or bioengineering may very well lead to 'data colonialism' or 'digital dictatorships', which unlike their predecessors will utilise algorithmic advantage to restructure entire societies and usher in a dystopian future of surveillance control for the world's most vulnerable populations.
> (Rozpedowski, 2021).

As time has passed, compulsive interest for the accumulation of consumerism in almost everything we produce and do with art, especially technologically, is indisputably shaping our collaborations online, mainly because it is run by the social hierarchy where profit becomes the main incentive for elitists who run technological platforms. Currently, uses for technology can create questions about art's monetary motive online through passive present-day technological art movements, which was not so apparent in Cybernetics Art or Network Art. Today's construct of technology is also very automated, as noted in an interview by Emily Gosling with Olia Lialina, an innovating artist who was an adopter of Network Art as a medium as early as 1997; she mentions the current ways we interact with technology, saying:

> Today website design is so much more accessible. It means you have to do less and less, but for me, that's killing the personality of websites. It makes you alienated from the design and coding part.
>
> (Gosling, 2020)

This means it is 'killing the personality of websites' and the human creativity behind the computer screen in pioneering movements like Net Art, slowly deteriorating creativity due to overly accessible readymade ideas and aesthetics adaptable online today.

Chapter 2

Women, Technology and Art

As we undoubtedly exist amongst an ingrained hierarchy of social structures, recognition of this is a crucial concept within this thesis; the internet and technology are no different. They are placing males' ideas, advancements and understanding of technology at the forefront, which we see ubiquitously. This predetermined social structure affects gender visibility, wealth, and inequity, firmly recognised by the great female writer Virginia Woolf, who is quoted, "In the arts, women's productions have been ignored so often that they have been virtually invisible, leading Virginia Woolf to conclude that Anonymous must have been woman" (Lorber, 2009, p.6).

Just as technological use and advancements are ubiquitous, so too is the male logic that consequently attaches and burrows in everything we do, making it a frequent fact that we fall victim to inequity online or through technology, as noted here in the book *Reflections on Gender and Technology Studies: In What State is the Art?* by Judy Wajcman who states, "After all, if technologies are inscribed with gender relations in their design, then the culture of computing is predominantly the culture of the white American" (Wajcman, 2000, p. 459).

Equality in the art world does not align as it should within the genders, especially in our current modernity with technological machinery, where technology seems to be coined explicitly for male interaction and be educated primarily for males, thus creating further gaps in the apparent race for a virtual life. Thus, the gap is further widening as male technological occupations do, disregarding women in the industry. Where we can see the epitome of inequality still thriving, as it generally does, within genders is regrettably within the arts. This deep-rooted hierarchy establishes theories on why this may be, and this is not classified information. Since the beginning, we know women artists have not had the same coverage and respectability according to how their male colleagues have been received in the arts, causing inevitable disparity when it comes to payment of artworks made by women, as has recently been discussed throughout the world's press following the BBC Radio 4 documentary, *Recalculating Art*. Here, Helen Gorrill appeared alongside the Tate Director Frances Morris, and referring to her book *Women Can't Paint*, she clarified that there is currently a 10:1 gender pay gap in contemporary art sales – that is, that for every £1 a man earns when he sells a work of art, women (on average) earn just 10p (Gorrill 2020).

Technology plays a part in widening this inequality; by adding barriers in technological developments and coverage for women; this lack dims the excellence of many influential and vital women who played enormous roles in the story within technological advancements in the arts. Recognition of women from the beginning with art and technology is essential; it helps grasp the fact that their roles in the passages of technological encounters in art also came from women and are not new as we see in the 1968 exhibition *Cybernetics Serendipity* with curator Jasia Reichardt and exhibition designer Franciszka Themerson, previously mentioned in chapter one (Malloy, 2003). Acknowledging women's input also helps to change how we think about the past and future encounters for women in the arts whowork with technology, thus helping to replace stigma with veracity. The *Leonardo* Women, Art and Technology Project helps vanguard women and their important works of art that show their interaction and innovation with technology, as "The *Leonardo* Women, Art and Technology Project began in 1993 to encourage women artists working with technology-based media to write about their work" (Malloy, 2003, p.13). The book published by Leonardo called *Women, Art, and Technology* edited by Judy Malloy, shows extensive ways in which women have interacted as well as pioneered the arts and technology in earlier times; it mentions artists such as Rebecca Allen, who is still known today for her work with technology and presently creates with technological mediums. In the book by Leonardo reads a section in bold that is fitting regarding the stigma around conditions for women in the world of technology, which states "I Always Like to Go Where I Am Not Supposed to Be" (Malloy, 2003, p.224) and cites an interview held by Erkki Huhtamo with Rebecca Allen. In this interview, we can admire the drive that helped hold Allen as an innovator and pioneer of early uses for technology in art and her ability to recognise in earlier years that technology would become a big part of our society as she mentions in the interview when asked by Erkki how she got involved in technology and art:

> RA: "As I began to think of technologies of our time and their impact, I recognised that computers would become an important part of society and could be important tools for artists as well." (Malloy, 2003, p.225)

Rebecca Allen recognised this protentional in technology as a tool as did other women in the art world; it is written that she "Began to explore the possibilities of digital technology in the early 1970s when most people hardly knew what a computer was" (Malloy, 2003, p.225).

A work more recently created with further development in interactive technologies by Allen is the work called 'Chamber of Mirrors' built-in 2011 (Rebecca Allen, 2011); this work is alluring and attractive in the sense that it does not dissociate the importance of physical interaction of human-to-human experience, as technology presently strives for, nor does it isolate you behind a technological device as described here:

> Most of today's social media and gaming happens in front of a screen with no connection to our physical surroundings and lacking the richness of face-to-face socialising. This game takes place in the "real world" with a group of people.
>
> (Rebecca Allen, n. d).

With this, it is clear that Allen understood the dangers of technologies' isolating qualities, a reason for contention around technology today; with this work, she intended to change this, something not often thought about when interacting and developing technology today.

Some changes in women's roles and how women were perceived with technology in the arts in our hierarchical society can be seen in 'Documenta X', the 10th Documenta in Kassel 1997 (Documenta, 1997); this particular Documenta appointed the first women director ever, who was Catherine David. 'Documenta X' featured many influential artists who worked with technology, and many women showed their expertise in the level of male's abilities to work with technology and art. Jodi, a duo formed of Joan Heemskerk and Dirk Paesmans is seen as being an effective technological collaboration who showed innovation in the age of advancements with the Internet. It was noted that they "pioneered Web art in the mid-1990s" (net-art.org, n.d) and "Jodi were among the first artists to investigate and subvert conventions of the Internet, computer programmes and video and computer games" (net-art.org, n. d).

Likewise, we should recognise the work and creative 'Cyberfeminism' ideas of the *Old Boys Network,* also known as 'OBN' (monoskop.org, 2021). This included eight female members who created "real and virtual spaces where Cyberfeminists can research, experiment, communicate and act" (monoskop.org, 2021). Furthermore, they stated that "The OBN platforms aim to provide a contextualised presence for the diverse and interdisciplinary approaches to Cyberfeminism" (monoskop.org, 2021). The OBN had a space at 'Documenta X' noted by Obn.org, that operated from 20th of September to 28th in 1997, it continued from 1997 to 2001 (Obn.org, 2021). Talent and innovation in the technological arts by women is not all unnoticed; there are successful, prominent women in the arts who work with technology today, such as Rachel MacLean, a Scottish artist who is well-received in the arts and a central figure for her video and installation works (Maclean, 2018). She uses different technology to produce "elaborate films and digital prints using costumes, exaggerated make-up, green screen visual effects and electronic soundtracks. Her work is titled *'Make Me Up'* (Maclean, Rachel, 2018). The work is a video, which includes Rachel MacLean herself in a world that holds a dark presence of ferocity and dictatorship of privacy for women within the video work (Maclean, 2018).

Her respected place in the art world has not gone unnoticed. She has showcased her work worldwide, representing Scotland, her home country, at the renowned art event Venice Biennale (Nationalgalleries.org, 2017) - a tremendous achievement. Unfortunately, even with some recognition for women who create with technology such as Rachel Maclean has received, there is still inequality and a lack of female presence generally with technology, which undoubtedly affects how many women also use technology as a medium in the arts and how they decide whether they want to learn about technology, as well as how much they earn from it. Presently, this inequality is noted in a report produced in 2021 by the United Nations Conference on Trade and Development:

> Currently most technologies are created by firms in the global North and predominantly by men. They tend to focus on the demands of the rich, crowding out innovations that might benefit the poor. Technological change is also shaped by gender inequalities, partly because men have been more likely than women to study STEM subjects.
>
> (United Nations, 2021, p. 21).

We, in conclusion, will not see a significant change in the perception of women working with technology, be it as an occupational business side or as an artist, if this deep-rooted divide remains following the social hierarchy that perpetuates a climate in which women predominately steer clear of learning and interacting with STEM subjects, due to how women have been perceived in this social structure that predetermines where they 'acceptably' belong. New crazes with technology, such as Crypto Art that uses NFT technology, grew intensely popular in 2021. NFTs are short for non-fungible tokens, and typically this is a digitally created and perceived artwork that ties to cryptocurrency.

Art, Inequity and Technological Ubiquity

Previously noted by Artsy.net, and the graphs presented in Helen Gorrill's 2020 book Women Can't Paint which were compiled about inequality in sales, the gender divide is currently apparent in technology and art here too as "female artists account for only 5% of all NFT Art sales" (Arvelaiz, 2021). With this being a newer technological art form, it depicts that not much change has happened in the past 21 months regarding women's respectability in the technological art scene (Arvelaiz, 2021). As we progress technologically within art mediums such as this heightened use for NFT's that will be further discussed within the last chapter, we furthermore still seem to only recognise and broaden the importance of wealthy male figures and favour their works, as we have seen throughout technology, not to forget a large section of humanity generally, as noted in the report by the United Nations that "Many developing countries lack adequate digital infrastructure, and for most of their people Internet costs are prohibitive" (United Nations, 2021, p. 22). Subsequently, this leaves out a large proportion of the world generally in technological advancements, never mind in cryptocurrencies, virtual, living, or just women.

Chapter 3

Connecting to Contemporary Art and Technology Movements

"Any radically new, Pioneering generation of demands will go too far"

(Benjamin, 2008, p.43)

As Walter Benjamin states in the above quotation in his book originally published in 1936, his realisation that demands will go too far is now apparent as we can now see how this has become accurate; the writer and American poet Wendell Berry writes on this furthering demand, the cycle of dependability and the ingrained need for consumerism with technology. He touches on the unfortunate truth that we always look for the most up-to-date technological products. This only furthers corporations' hold on us because he believes:

> The future, thanks only to more purchasable products, is going to be even better. Thus, consumers become salesmen, and the world is made safer for corporations.
>
> (Berry, 2018, p.10).

Berry's sarcastic tone in his depiction of the reality of the dangers of the mass production and need for consuming that society has ingrained is deliberate. Paul Virilio talks about a similarly worrying observation in his book *Ground Zero*, reflecting the effects through art; he argues that with :

> constant acceleration of technologies' presentation and reproduction both dromological and dromoscopic which, by reducing the space and time between subject and object to zero, were to eliminate, as a matter of course, not just the concepts of rarity and *durée,* but the *nodal points of the potentiality and the 'becoming' of the work of art* – its phenomenology

(Virilio, 2002, p.51).

Understanding the accelerating speed in which technology can work and its ability to reproduce decreases the distance between us and the actual works of art by looking at reproduced states online, changing our experience by not physically seeing the work.

Reproducing artwork online can disregard the intentions of the artist's work and its intended medium by changing its materiality into tiny pixels rather than being physically viewed. This change in intention can be recognised in postmodern art; using technology to view art online was not considered before these technological advancements, changing how the artists thought their work would be viewed. The Tate defines aura as "a quality integral to an artwork that cannot be communicated through mechanical reproduction techniques – such as photography" (Tate.org, n. d), something the internet largely favours with a readily available overload of images.

This possibility of exposure to auratic properties and essences of arts and history have been observed by Catherine Cameron and John Gatewood, suggesting the importance of indulging in physical reality with history, art and culture sites to expose what they would call 'numinous experiences':

> Not only do people visit museums to seek a form of transcendent experience, but historic sites and exhibits can conjure emotional responses that link museum visitors to a historical past. They described a framework for analysing what they termed "numinous experiences" characterised by three traits: deep engagement or transcendence, empathy through affective connection, and awe or reverence akin to spiritual communion.
>
> (Cameron & Gatewood, 2018, p.280).

The above text depicts the challenges of viewing art online, prompting why viewing artwork in a real-life physical space, especially historical work by artists such as Mark Rothko, is essential to submerge yourself in the essence of the work as he noted "I also hang the largest pictures so that they must be first encountered at close quarters, so that the first experience is to be within the picture" (National Gallery of Art, n. d). The sheer size of Rothko's works cannot be comprehended into a readily formatted version by pixels online nor was it intended for that. First-hand encounters externally and physically are where it can be strongly argued that one may grasp a transcending experience, as Mark Rothko once said; "A painting is not a picture of an experience; it is an experience" (quoted in Twemlow, 2013).

This increased change in how we perceive and view art and its phenomenology, as Virilio mentioned, is similarly spoken about by Walter Benjamin, as he delves into the aura of an artwork and its lack of uniqueness through mass reproduction. He predominately links this to films and photography, a mass reproduced art form. However, his theories on this subject undoubtedly cross over and shape how we interact and feel about art through technological means such as the internet and digitalisation of art online. Walter Benjamin writes that "Even with the most perfect reproduction, one thing stands out: the here and now of the work of art – its unique existence in the place where it is at this moment" (Benjamin, 2008, p.5). Thus, the idea highlights that the reproduced state of the art does not hold a uniqueness in which the original bares, this uniqueness that stands only within the original through itself and its history of existence physically on this planet. He then goes on to write that "We can say: what shrinks in the age where the work of art can be reproduced by technological means is its 'aura' (Benjamin, 2008, p.7).

With the current pandemic, as educational learning and university classes go online, so too did art galleries and interactions online through technological means branded to "stop the spread" (stopthespread.org, 2021) of Covid-19 through decreasing physicality in our external world that encouraged virtual viewing. Our physical experiences with art have decreased, questioning our exposure to artworks' auras, thus bringing forth the question of how future generations may interact with past art if technology and a virtual life take over, as we see is becoming more and more apparent. The online galleries did not originate from the advice to stay home during the pandemic in 2021; however, their presence has only grown more prominent with this (Rowe, 2021).

Enabling art to be widespread online helps bring interest and learning around art in developed countries, undeniably. However, growth with online use forwards dependability and exclusion for those not able to access technological means, such as the internet, marginalising oppressed groups further.

Movements such as the Crypto art scene show where exclusion within the arts playout. NFTs have made a pixelated state of digital images part of the aesthetic of the art form. Many crypto artworks, such as 'Bored Ape Yacht Club' are digitally perceived (Perper, R., 2021), so it can be argued this fits the intention of some artists. However, this craze over digital works of art exposes the division between who can afford to interact with the art.

Crypto Art is a digital piece of art with monetary value and ownership through NFTs and cryptocurrency, branded that it is "unique and can't be replaced with something else" (Clark, 2021). The idea that these are "unique and can't be replaced with something else" seemingly implies further capitalisation of the art world; a brand slogan in the race to be one of a kind (Clark, 2021). Crypto Art and NFTs are sought after within the emerging elitist online world, with many A-listers buying them as an intended extension of themselves virtually; this can be comprehended as prodigal and capitalising as it becomes an investment rather than a gratifying work of art that can be physically viewed. Monetary gain within art is not a new attraction; however, Crypto Art increases the division between social classes. Making money with this type of art relies on the fact that one must know what one is doing with investment. Secondly, cryptocurrencies are complex, let alone in art; it can be difficult, if not impossible, in some cases, to grasp.

Artists and clueless buyers have lost profit using this art form. Million-pound success stories usually come from people with prior knowledge of cryptocurrencies and investing, thus again pinpointing the already existing social inequalities. Crypto Art, therefore, ultimately favours the rich who understand and have access to money and technological equipment required to invest in it (Clark, 2021).

This issue was discussed by BBC technology reporter, Cristina Criddle, talking about her experience with buying a crypto work of art:

> My first experience of investing in this world was a nightmare - with far too much time, money and stress wasted on… well, not very much. Because an NFT doesn't have a physical representation like a painting, it exists only as a digital asset.
>
> (Criddle, 2021)

As seen above, buying Crypto Art can leave owners of the works impassive with the process as well as the art itself; it is undisclosed information that ultimately with these digital-based crypto artworks. Furthermore, people who do not own the works can undoubtedly save them virtually on almost any device as has been done with the 'Bored Ape Yacht Club', making it ever more ludicrous how expensive the Crypto Art market is regarding these types of works, so that wasting a fair amount of time, effort and money to own one is incomprehensible.

The extensive furthering of climate change is where the excessive use of technology and Crypto Art causes disaster; it perpetuates the need for a communal concern on current technological advancements in art. The technological Crypto Art movement is questionable in its shift of how art is perceived and its furthering of capitalisation. Still, the excess energy required to produce, sell, and buy the works is alarming, especially when excessive power is used to fuel technological use such as the social media spectacle already being consumed everywhere. Crypto Art and cryptocurrencies may not be the biggest reason for the warming of the planet but are partially responsible, thus making it not only fruitless within the art world in terms of its concept and materiality - but also its futile need to be created in the first instance when it has damaging effects on the planet. "Individual pieces of crypto art, non-fungible tokens (NFTs), are at least partially responsible for the millions of tons of planet-heating carbon dioxide emissions generated by the cryptocurrencies used to buy and sell them" (Calma, 2021). Recognition of its negative qualities on earth is known, likewise in a book written in 2018 it is noted Cryptocurrencies, like Bitcoin, "Requires the energy of nine US homes to perform a single transaction; and if its growth continues, by 2019 it will require the annual power output of the entire United States to sustain itself" (Bridle, 2018, p. 29), something we can see has played out with rapid growth only furthered by a crypto art craze, facilitating the excessive energy use that worsens the climate crisis. Technology acts as a catalyst for climate change – it is its own worst enemy, an opinion infrequently thought about in art forms that accelerate it. It will eventually make itself redundant; our technology on earth was not built to last in harsh climate conditions. In trying to monitor an ever-changing climate, technology will be forced to upgrade for the degradation of the earth continually. In other words, "The systems we have built to collapse time and space are being attacked by time and space" (Bridle, 2018, p.28). With all this being said, some changes can be made to make the process of buying Crypto Art and cryptocurrencies less damaging to our planet with changes to how Ethereum and Bitcoin work, two recognised cryptocurrencies used to buy Crypto NFT Art. These secure and keep tabs working like a 'receipt' through a blockchain process called 'proof of work', which uses masses of energy to ensure records of transactions.

> *Similarly, blockchains used within NFTs work like banks, keeping money secure and legitimising transactions. Currently, they are noted as being high energy consumers purposefully, as "The idea is that using*

up inordinate amounts of electricity — and probably paying a lot for it — makes it less profitable for someone to muck up the ledger" (Calma, 2021). The damaging effects are undeniable:

"This usage creates negative social externalities, most significantly by contributing to climate change and impacting human health from the burning of fossil fuels. It was recently argued that CO_2 emissions from Bitcoin mining alone could push global warming above the 2 °C threshold of concern" (Goodkind, A. et al., 2019).

There are greener ways to secure NFTs and cryptocurrency; Ethereum has been talking about using a lighter way to secure transactions using proof of stake, more environmentally-friendly than proof of work. However, this has not happened yet, meaning we need to change urgently how we buy and create Crypto Art, NFTs and cryptocurrency by gathering a better understanding of their environmental impact (Calma, 2021). As the Crypto Art craze worsens, so too does this excessive energy use and compulsion to buy and own Crypto Art. Ownership of these artworks builds the picture of humanity's flaw to be excessively unique owners, heightened by materialistic tendencies, making this type of art thrive in the name of consumerism driven by capitalism and benefiting those who govern it.

Conclusion

This book has explored in three chapters some ways in which mechanical and electronic technological advancement in humanity have been used in the arts in ground-breaking ways. Yet, irresponsible use has furthered inequity in art and, generally, changed how we experience the art world. Virtualised art can decrease exposure to auratic experiences and growing greed for monetary gain as a capitalist society strives for this. It uses an overbearing system favouring the hierarchy, furthering gender discrimination and contributing to climate degradation. This submits the art world to an ethical paradox with ever-exceeding conflicts and sheds light on the deeper global issue of growth in an unfulfilling, depressing reality of existence if personal and global uses are unregulated. This thesis has revealed some behavioural impacts of technology upon the psyche with improper use and aims to raise awareness and understanding of how to start changing our relationship with technology. As art falls victim to technological services presently, just as branches of life do, an excessive technological world favours the elite, creating a never-ending cycle of mass production to consume and capitalise. Suppose changes are not made upon overbearing knowledge of the adverse effects of technology misuse, the rich will grow richer; as clichéd as it may sound, the system that prioritises profit rather than happiness is conditioned under capitalism, allows the hierarchy to remain in place. Will art become out of reach for those excluded from society's pecking order, and will arts and culture fully become commodities? Technology is not problematic alone however, it has been developed so that those who control the knowledge surrounding it bask in beneficial uses; if knowledge and uses are not evenly distributed, art will remain chained to the bourgeoisie as it moves to ubiquitous technological use. It is undeniable that greatness has arrived due to technological uses in the past and present. Although its future is mysterious amongst our conditioning use within our social and economic structure, it depicts a reality that is bleak. The ever-present idea is that gratitude for what we have slows capitalism because we do not need or want more, posing desolate realities that further follow the capitalist society, furthered by technological means (Haig, 2015).

Joslyn Lundie

Bibliography

Alegria, S.N. (2020) 'What do we mean by broadening participation? Race, inequality, and diversity in tech work', Sociology compass, 14(6). doi:10.1111/soc4.12793. (Accessed 27 November 2021).

Arvelaiz, J. (2021) *It's a Man's Market: NFT Female Artists Made 5% Of Sales in 21 Months*. Available at: https://www.newsbtc.com/nft/its-a-mans-market-nft-female-artist-made-5-of-sales-in-21-months/ (Accessed: 8 December 2021).

Benjamin, W. (2008) *The Work of Art in the Age of Mechanical Reproduction*. London: The Penguin Group.

Berry, W. (2018) *Why I am Not Going to Buy a Computer*. London: Penguin Books.

Bridle, J. (2018) New Dark Age: Technology and the End of the Future. London: Verso.

Calma, J. (2021) *The climate controversy swirling around NFTS*. Available at: https://www.theverge.com/2021/3/15/22328203/nft-cryptoart-ethereum-blockchain-climate-change (Accessed: 8 January 2022).

Clark, M. (2021) *NFT's, Explained*. Available at:https://www.theverge.com/22310188/nftexplainer-what-is-blockchain-crypto-art-faq (Accessed: 8 January 2022).

Corby, Tom. 2006. *Network Art: Practices and Positions*. Abingdon, Oxon: Routledge. (Accessed on 23 November 2021).

Criddle, C. (2021) *Buying a Pink NFT cat was a crypto nightmare*. Available at: https://www.bbc.co.uk/news/technology-57273904 (Accessed: 8 January 2022).

Dalgarno, E. (2001) *Virginia Woolf and the visible world.*. Cambridge: Cambridge University Press.

Documenta (n. d) *Documenta X*. Available at: https://www.documenta.de/en/retrospective/documenta_x (Accessed: 6 December 2021).

Evans-Pughe, C. (2018) *Cybernetics Serendipity: Did 60's art shape technology's future?*. Available at: https://eandt.theiet.org/content/articles/2018/04/cybernetic-serendipity-did-60s-art-shape-technology-s-future/(Accessed: 21 November 2021).

Fai, Cao. (Unknown) *Works*. Available at: http://www.caofei.com/works.aspx?id=79&year=2018&wtid=3 (Accessed: 8 January 2022).

Fei, Cao. (Unknown) *About*. Available at: http://www.caofei.com/about.aspx (Accessed: 2 January 2022).

Gazzaley, A. and Rosen.d, L. (2016) The Distracted Mind: *Ancient Brains in a High-Tech World*. Rochester: MIT Press.

Goodkind, A. et al., (2019) Cryptodamages: Monetary value estimates of the air pollution and human health impacts of cryptocurrency mining. Available at: https://www.sciencedirect.com/science/article/pii/S2214629619302701 (Accessed: 8 January 2022)

Gorrill, H. (2019) *Women can't paint: gender, the glass ceiling and values in contemporary art.* New York: Bloomsbury Publishing.

Gosling, Emily. (2020) What Does Net Art Mean in the Post-Digital Age?. Available at: https://elephant.art/what-does-net-art-mean-in-the-post-digital-age-olia-lialina-30032020/ (20 December 2021).

Haig, M. (2015) *Reasons to Stay Alive.* Edinburgh: Canongate.

Haig, M. (2019) Notes on a nervous planet. Edinburgh: Canongate.

Lorber, J. (2009) Gender Inequality: Feminist Theories and Politics. Oxford: Oxford University Press. Edition: 4.

Maclean, Rachel (n. d) Make Me Up. Available at: http://www.rachelmaclean.com/make-me-up-film/ (Accessed: 7 December 2021).

Malloy, J. (2003) Women, art, and technology. Cambridge, Massachusetts: MIT Press.

Margulis, A., Boeck, H. and Laroche, M. (2020) 'Connecting with consumers using ubiquitous technology: A new model to forecast consumer reaction', Journal of business research, 121, pp. 448–460. doi:10.1016/j.jbusres.2019.04.019.

Mason, Catherine. (2018) Cybernetic Serendipity: History and Lasting Legacy. *StudioInternational*. Available at:https://www.studiointernational.com/index.php/cybernetic-serendipity-history-and-lasting-legacy. (Accessed on 18 November 2021).

monoskop.org (2021) Old Boys Network. Available at: https://monoskop.org/Old_Boys_Network#Publications (Accessed: 7 December 2021).

Mudam (2021) Post-Capital: Art and the Economics of the Digital Age. Available at: https://www.mudam.com/exhibitions/post-capital (Accessed: 3 January 2022).

National Gallery of Art (n. d) *Mark Rothko: Classic Paintings*. Available at: https://www.nga.gov/features/mark-rothko/mark-rothko-classic-paintings.html (Accessed: 3 January 2021).

Nationalgalleries.org (2017) Rachel Maclean. Available at: https://www.nationalgalleries.org/art-and-artists/artists/rachel-maclean (Accessed: 8 December 2021).

net-art.org, (n. d) Jodi. Available at: https://net-art.org/jodi-0 (Accessed: 6 December 2021).

Nugent, Annabel. 2020. UK adults spend 40% of waking hours in front of a screen, study finds. *The Independent*. Available at: https://www.independent.co.uk/arts-entertainment/tv/news/screen-time-average-uk-study-ofcom-a9654546.html. (Accessed on 18 November 2021).

Obn.org (2021) Cyberfeminist International. Available at: https://obn.org/obn/obn_pro/kassel/index.html (Accessed: 7 December 2021).

Paul, C. (2006) First Monday. Available at: https://firstmonday.org/ojs/index.php/fm/article/view/1616/1531 (Accessed: 23 November 2021).

Perper, R. (2021) A $300,000 USD Bored Ape NFT Accidentally Sold for $3,000 USD Because of a Typo. Available at: https://hypebeast.com/2021/12/bored-ape-yacht-club-nft-typo-sold-3000-mistake-listing (Accessed: 6 January 2021).

Reichardt, Jasia. 2014. Cybernetic Serendipity: A Documentation. Institute of Contemporary Art. *Fox Reading Room*. Available at: https://archive.ica.art/whats-on/cybernetic-serendipity-documentation/. (Accessed on 18 November 2021)

Routledge (2018) The Routledge Handbook of Museums, Media and Communication. Oxfordshire: Routledge (Accessed: 17 December 2021).

Rowe, M. (2021) Will The increase of Online Exhibitions kill the physical gallery?. Available at: https://www.theguardian.com/artanddesign/2021/oct/14/online-exhibitions-art-galleries (Accessed: 8 January 2021).

Rozpedowski, Joanna. 2021. Digital Sovereignty in an Era of Global Surveillance, Disinformation, and Info-demics | Geopolitical Monitor. GeopoliticalMonitor.com. Available at:

https://www.geopoliticalmonitor.com/digital-sovereignty-in-an-era-of-global-surveillance-disinformation-and-info-demics/ (Accessed 29 November 2021).

Steyerl, H. (2017) Duty Free Art: Art in the Age of Planetary Civil War. London: Verso.

stopthespread.org (2021) *Stop The Spread*. Available at: https://www.stopthespread.org/ (Accessed: 8 January 2021).

Stryker, Beth and Brooks, Sawad. 2005. *PORTFOLIO | | Sawad Brooks*. Open-work.com. Available at: http://www.open-work.com/sawad/portfolio/general/ (Accessed 28 November 2021).

Stryker, Beth and Brooks, Sawad. n.d. *disseminet.walkerart.org*. Disseminet.walkerart.org. Available at: http://disseminet.walkerart.org/html/gallerycredits.html (Accessed 28 November 2021).

Tate.org (n. d) Aura - Art Term. Available at: https://www.tate.org.uk/art/art-terms/a/aura (Accessed: 10 December 2021).

Tunali, Tijen. 2016. Studies in Visual Arts and Communications: an international journal Vol 3, No 1 (2016) on-line ISSN 2393 - 1221) Available at: https://net-art.org/net-art-and-activism. (Accessed 23 November 2021).

Twemlow, M. (2013) A Painting as An Experience. Available at: https://www.metmuseum.org/blogs/teen-blog/modern-and-contemporary/posts/rothko(Accessed: 5 January 2021).

United Nations (2021) Technology and Innovation Report 2021. Place of publication: New York Available at: https://unctad.org/system/files/official-document/tir2020_en.pdf (Accessed: 8 December 2021).

Virilio, P. (2002) Ground Zero. London: Verso.

Wajcman, J. (2000) 'Reflections on Gender and Technology Studies: In What State is the Art?', Social studies of science, 30(3). doi:10.1177/030631200030003005.

Joslyn Lundie

Artist's images

Joslyn Lundie

Art, Inequity and Technological Ubiquity

For the Duncan of Jordanstone College of Art & Designs 2022 Degree Show, Joslyn created a wall-based installation - constructed of 22 glass panels and photographic baggage scans from airport security, directing viewers to a deeper understanding of current control societies based on the writings of French philosopher Gilles Deleuze. Each glass panel has been assigned 1 red box, representing an Explosive detection system (EDS) flagged area. Thus, creating an EDS mapped language system, allowing the viewer to translate the censored message installed on the gallery wall, by following a provided key. In a controlled society; humans are no longer individuals requiring discipline, but rather, dividual sources of information traced and amalgamated by technological ability and surveillance. This work explores controlled environments today that normalise the exposure of one's belongings and identity, moving from conventional speech to machine-based learning. EDS technology processes and identifies when density thresholds of baggage are surpassed, implementing limitations and invading passengers' privacy, whilst dictating the tasks that security staff must carry out to search flagged areas of luggage. The exercise of revealing the concealed message within the gallery space, draws attention to the confinements of regulation experienced by individuals, imposing a mechanistic dividual agenda that must be adhered to when exposing the hidden text.

This work consisted of a wall-based installation and a foldable paper zine of the alphabet created during this project. Thus, allowing the text to be uncovered and allow those to use this alphabet system to create their own hidden messages.

The following images portray Joslyn Lund's degree show installation, from the 2022 DJCAD annual exhibition. For further information and enquiries, please contact Joslyn at joslynlundie007@gmail.com. You can also follow Joslyn on Instagram, @joslynlundieart.

Art, Inequity and Technological Ubiquity

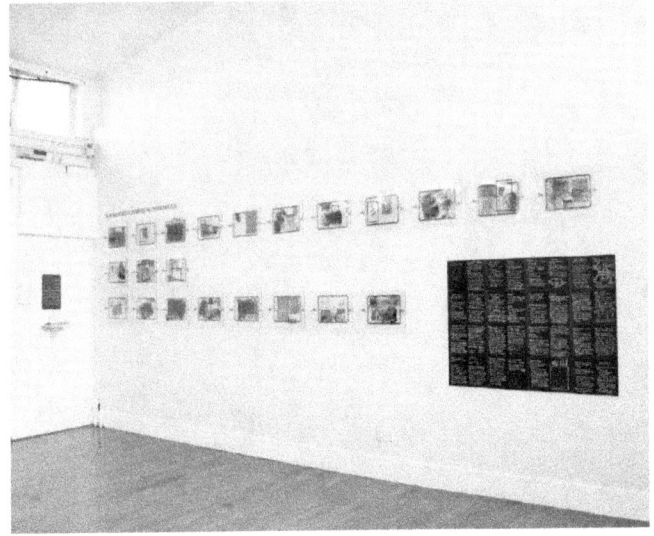

Joslyn Lundie

Art, Inequity and Technological Ubiquity

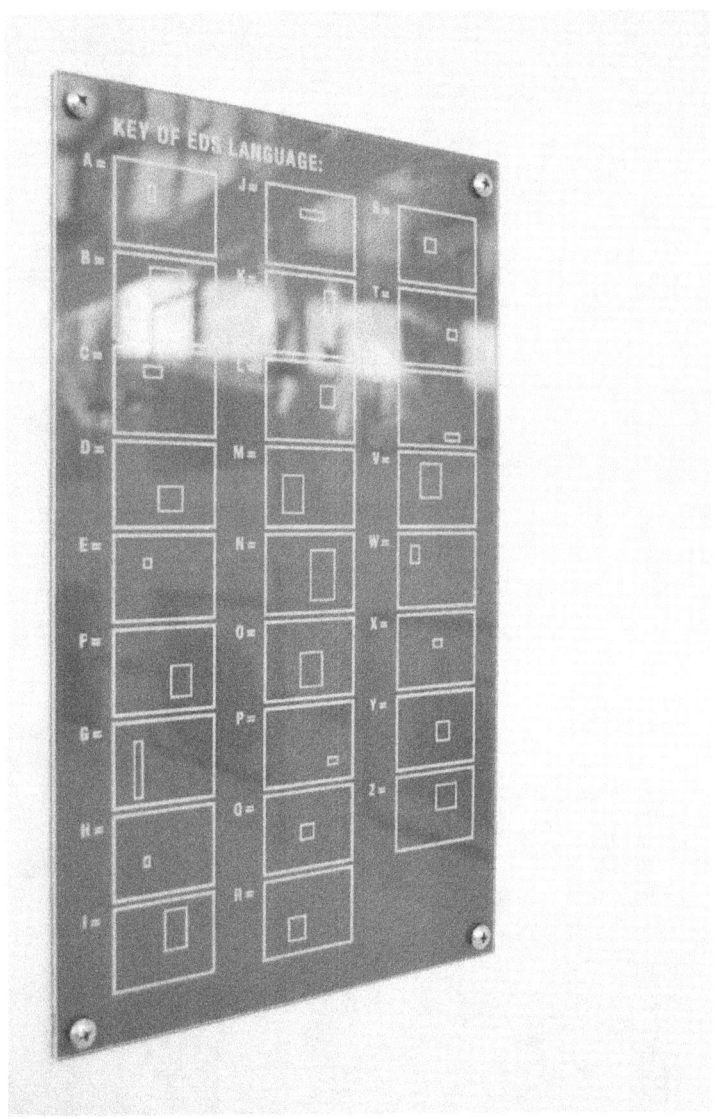

Joslyn Lundie

Art, Inequity and Technological Ubiquity

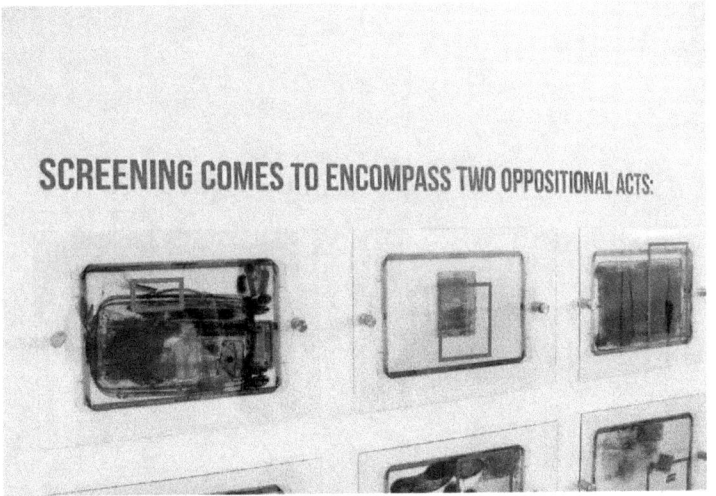

Joslyn Lundie

Art, Inequity and Technological Ubiquity

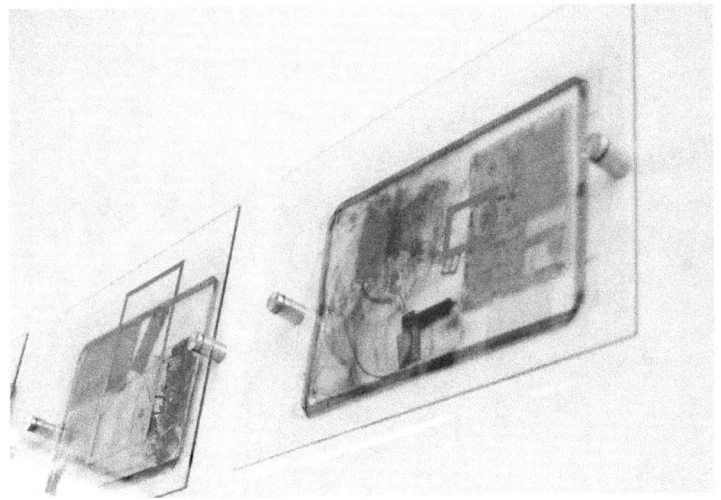

Joslyn Lundie

Acknowledgements

I would like to show gratification for the support and time given by my advisor, Dr Anna Notaro. Her support helped me to recognise the importance of the journey of learning.

I would also like to add my gratitude to my aunt, Bernice Avery Borain who supported me throughout this writing. Her support was invaluable, and her knowledge is admirable.

Lastly, I would like to acknowledge the support given by my family and friends. Their cordiality supported me in more ways than imaginable throughout the research, writing and editing processes aiding the completion of this writing.

Joslyn Lundie

A note about Boom Graduates

We propel graduates forward so they can make their mark on the world - we push the boundaries, share brilliant ideas and inspire possibility. We publish dissertations as books, presented gift-boxed at graduation ceremonies, delivering brand-new research to the world quicker than anyone else. We plant trees for every commissioned book sold, and give our Boom graduates the chance to profit-share from their brilliant ideas. Furthermore we donate the majority of our profits to funding research and scholarship for disadvantaged students who wouldn't normally be able to attend university. Through academic excellence and environmental sustainability, *Boom Graduates* are changing the world.

We are Boom Graduates - an imprint of Boom Publications Ltd. We are a more-than-profit company, dedicating over half our profits to providing university scholarships for underprivileged students across the world. We aim to become the globe's biggest provider of such scholarships – and if like Joslyn, the author of this book, you'd also like to contribute to making the world a better place, please contact us: we publish monographs, edited books, and moreover our graduate series – Boom Graduates – are presented at graduation days across the world in archival, lined museum-quality presentation cases, engraved with the graduate's name and award.

Boom Publications are based at the Duncan of Jordanstone College of Art and Design, at the University of Dundee in Scotland. We were one of the winners of the 2022 Venture awards hosted by the Centre for Entrepreneurship, and have since been shortlisted for the Converge Challenge, a national award that brings together ambitious and creative thinkers with innovative ideas to work with industry experts to transform their ideas into sustainable companies operating in the commercial world. We are also climate conscious and work with agencies to plant a tree for each and every book commissioned, offsetting thousands of tonnes of carbon each year. Follow us on social media to watch our forest grow @boomgraduates.

Thank you for contributing by purchasing this book. Please visit our catalogues on www.boompublications.com.

BOOM!

This book was originally submitted as a dissertation in partial fulfilment of the requirements of a Bachelor of Arts (Hons) degree in Fine Art at the Duncan of Jordanstone College of Art and Design, the University of Dundee, in 2022.

Joslyn Lundie

Notes

Joslyn Lundie

Art, Inequity and Technological Ubiquity

Joslyn Lundie

Art, Inequity and Technological Ubiquity

Joslyn Lundie

Art, Inequity and Technological Ubiquity

Joslyn Lundie

Art, Inequity and Technological Ubiquity

Joslyn Lundie

Art, Inequity and Technological Ubiquity

www.ingramcontent.com/pod-product-compliance
Lightning Source LLC
Chambersburg PA
CBHW050243220526
45465CB00002B/534